BRITANNICA BEGINNER BIOS

WALT DISNEY

LEGENDARY ANIMATOR AND ENTERTAINMENT ENTREPRENEUR

JOSEPH KAMPFF

Britannica®
Educational Publishing

IN ASSOCIATION WITH

ROSEN
EDUCATIONAL SERVICES

Published in 2016 by Britannica Educational Publishing (a trademark of Encyclopædia Britannica, Inc.) in association with The Rosen Publishing Group, Inc.

29 East 21st Street, New York, NY 10010

Distributed exclusively by Rosen Publishing.

To see additional Britannica Educational Publishing titles, go to rosenpublishing.com.

First Edition

Britannica Educational Publishing
J.E. Luebering: Director, Core Reference Group
Mary Rose McCudden: Editor, Britannica Student Encyclopedia

Rosen Publishing
Christine Poolos: Editor
Nelson Sá: Art Director
Nicole Russo: Designer
Cindy Reiman: Photography Manager
Bruce Donnola: Photo Researcher

Library of Congress Cataloging-in-Publication Data

Kampff, Joseph.
 Walt Disney : legendary animator and entertainment entrepreneur / Joseph Kampff.
   pages cm. — (Britannica beginner bios)
 Includes bibliographical references and index.
 ISBN 978-1-68048-254-6 (library bound) — ISBN 978-1-5081-0059-1 (pbk.) -- ISBN 978-1-68048-312-3 (6-pack)
 1. Disney, Walt, 1901-1966—Juvenile literature. 2. Animators—United States—Biography—Juvenile literature. I. Title.
 NC1766.U52D54395 2005
 741.58092—dc23
 [B]

                                                                                              2015017786

Manufactured in the United States of America.

Photo Credits: Cover, pp. 1, 27 Alfred Eisenstaedt/The LIFE Picture Collection/Getty Images; p. 5 General Photographic Agency/Hulton Archive/Getty Images; pp. 7, 8 Apic/Hulton Archive/Getty Images; pp. 9, 11, 12, 19, 20 courtesy Everett Collection; p. 13 © Walt Disney Pictures/Ron Grant Archive/Alamy; p. 14 ullstein bild/Getty Images; p. 15 Photofest; pp. 16, 18, 24, 25 © AF archive/Alamy; p. 21 © Everett Collection Historical/Alamy; p. 23 © Walt Disney Pictures/courtesy Everett Collection; p. 26 Earl Theisen Collection/Archive Photos/Getty Images; interior pages background image Flame of life/Shutterstock.com

CONTENTS

CHAPTER ONE

THE MAN BEHIND THE MOUSE

It is almost impossible go through life without ever seeing something with the Disney name on it. Disney is everywhere. You probably know Mickey and Minnie Mouse, Donald Duck, Goofy, and Pluto. You might have been to Disneyland in California or Disney World in Florida. Maybe you watch the Disney Channel on television or visit the Disney Store at the mall. You might know every word to the song "Let It Go," from the Disney movie *Frozen* or watched the *Toy Story* movies over and over again.

What you might not know is that there is a real person behind all the cartoons, movies, and theme parks.

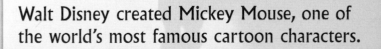

Walt Disney created Mickey Mouse, one of the world's most famous cartoon characters.

Quick Fact: Cartoons

People have been using pictures to tell stories for thousands of years. Long ago, artists drew on the walls of caves. In ancient Egypt, Greece, and Rome, artists painted on vases and walls. These pictures recorded historical events, legends, and the lives of important people.

Walt Disney is not just the name of a huge company. It is also the name of the person who started the Walt Disney Company. The man named Walt Disney created some of the most famous cartoon characters and movies in the world.

CHAPTER TWO

EARLY YEARS

Walt Disney's full name was Walter Elias Disney. He was born on December 5, 1901, in Chicago, Illinois. His father, Elias Disney, was a carpenter. Walt's mother, Flora, was a teacher. She left teaching to raise her family. The Disneys had four sons and one daughter. Walt was the youngest son.

Young Walt poses for a portrait with his little sister, Ruth, in 1906.

Walt's parents, Flora and Elias Disney, taught him the importance of hard work.

Walt's family moved to a farm in Missouri when he was very small. Walt loved life on the farm. He would ride on pigs and an old horse named Charley. Walt's older brothers helped their father with his work. Walt and his sister helped their mother. Because there was so much to do on the farm, Walt did not go to school until he was seven years old.

After Elias became sick and could

This photograph shows fourteen-year-old Walt at home in Kansas City, Missouri.

not run the farm, the family moved to Kansas City, Missouri. Elias took over a newspaper route and made Walt and his brother Roy deliver the papers. Walt also got his first job as an artist in Kansas City. Each week

Vocabulary Box

SKETCHES are quick, rough drawings that show the main features of an object, character, or scene.

he would do **SKETCHES** for a barber. He was paid either twenty-five cents for the sketches or given a haircut. Walt learned to work hard as a young boy. He continued to work hard all of his life.

But Walt did more than just work. He also loved to play and make people laugh. Walt always loved drawing pictures. He drew cartoon animals in the corners of his schoolbooks. When he flipped through the pages the animals looked like they were moving. It did not take

Quick Fact: Animation

Traditional animation involves filming a series of cartoon drawings to create the illusion of movement. Today, many animated films and television shows are made from computer-generated images.

Walt even drew a cartoon character on the ambulance he drove during World War I.

long for his teachers to recognize Walt's talent for drawing and painting.

The Disney family moved back to Chicago in 1917. Walt went to McKinley High School. He took photos and drew cartoons for the school paper. At night, he studied drawing at the Chicago Academy of Fine Art. Walt wanted to be a cartoonist for a newspaper. When he was sixteen, he signed up to be an ambulance driver in France during World War I.

CHAPTER THREE

FROM CARTOONS TO A STUDIO

Walt was almost eighteen years old when he returned home from the war. In 1919, he decided to go to Kansas City to become an artist. He had a few jobs drawing advertisements.

Disney found a job as a professional artist. Here, he is drawing advertisements in about 1920.

In 1922, Disney started Laugh-O-Gram Films. Soon afterward, he invited another artist named Ub Iwerks to join the company. Iwerks was a fantastic artist, and Disney was good at coming up with stories. Their biggest project was a series called the Alice Comedies that combined **LIVE-ACTION** and animation.

In 1923, Disney moved to Hollywood, California, and started a company with

> **Vocabulary Box**
>
> **LIVE-ACTION** refers to a movie or scene that uses actors and sets. Live-action movies are not produced by animation.

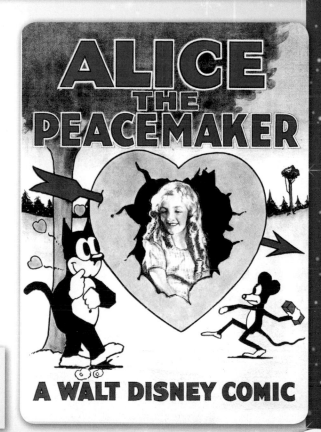

Alice the Peacemaker was one of Disney's Alice Comedies.

Walt Disney met Lillian Bounds at his own studios. They married and had a family.

his brother Roy called the Disney Brothers Studio. Disney brought Ub Iwerks to California to help out. They continued working on the Alice series. Disney also hired people to operate the cameras and work on animation. One of the people he hired was a woman named Lillian Bounds. Walt and Lillian fell in love and married in 1925.

Disney and Iwerks created a character named Oswald the Lucky Rabbit. Even though the character was popular, Disney's company was not able to make money from his cartoons. Disney and Iwerks

Ub Iwerks did much of the drawing for Walt Disney.

Mickey Mouse was silent in his first two cartoons. He was given a voice in *Steamboat Willie*.

had to come up with a new character fast.

In 1928, they came up with a new character that was a mouse. Disney wanted to call him Mortimer Mouse, but Lillian did not like that name. She talked him into changing the mouse's namc to Mickey. Mickey's sweetheart was named Minnie.

Mickey Mouse's first two cartoons, *Plane Crazy* and *Gallopin' Gaucho*, were never released. Mickey's third cartoon was called *Steamboat Willie* (1928). It was the first one that used sound. Disney hired an orchestra and even used his own voice for Mickey. *Steamboat Willie* was a huge success. People loved Mickey Mouse.

In 1929, Disney changed the name of his company to Walt Disney Productions. He also started a series of cartoons called Silly Symphonies. One of the cartoons in the series was *Flowers and Trees* (1932). It was the first cartoon ever made in full color. Disney added more characters to his cartoons. He came up with Donald Duck, Pluto, and Goofy.

CHAPTER FOUR

DISNEY MOVIES

Snow White and the Seven Dwarves is one of Walt Disney's most enduring films.

In 1934, Disney began his biggest project yet: *Snow White and the Seven Dwarves*. Disney had never made an animated film that was feature length. In fact, *Snow White* was the first feature-length animated film to use sound and color. Hundreds of people worked on the movie at great expense. *Snow White and the Seven Dwarves* was a box-office smash when it was released in 1937.

Disney made so much money from *Snow White* that he was able to build a brand new studio. It had the most up-to-date animation technology. Disney used the new studio to produce his next movie, *Pinocchio*. *Pinocchio* was released in 1940. Some consider it Disney's greatest achievement. *Pinocchio* is known for its brilliant animation and compelling story.

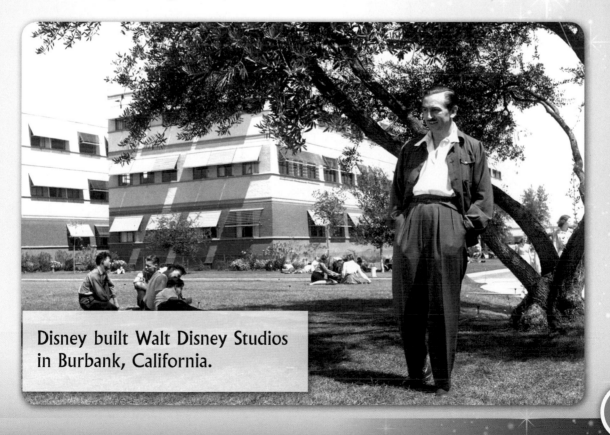

Disney built Walt Disney Studios in Burbank, California.

A **STRIKE** happens when employees stop working until their employer agrees to their demands. Workers on strike usually want better pay and improved working conditions.

By this time, hundreds of animators worked at Disney. Many of them felt they were not paid well, so in May 1941, Disney's animators went on **STRIKE**. Eventually, Roy Disney agreed to pay the workers more

Disney animators went on strike and demonstrated outside the Walt Disney Studios.

money. But Walt was not happy about this. He thought he was already paying them enough.

During World War II, Disney made movies for the U.S. government. These were usually train-ing films for soldiers going to war. Disney did not really enjoy making these kinds of movies. But he was able to make money from them. And he was happy to help the war effort.

Disney designed a Mickey Mouse gas mask to protect children from chemical warfare.

Quick Fact

Disney also released *Dumbo*, *Bambi*, and *Fantasia* in the early 1940s. These movies did not make as much money as *Snow White* had.

CHAPTER FIVE

BEYOND ANIMATION

After World War II, Disney realized he could make more money with live-action movies than with animated films. He first made movies using a combination of live-action and animation. These include *The Three Caballeros, Make Mine Music,* and *Song of the South.*

Disney's first fully live-action film was *Treasure Island.* It was released in 1950. The movie was based on a novel by Robert Louis Stevenson. It is about a young boy who goes off to find treasure with a group of pirates, including Long John Silver.

Television was still very new in the 1950s. Disney thought TV would be a good way to reach viewers. Disney's first TV production was called *One Hour in Wonderland.* It was shown on Christmas Day in 1950. In

Walt Disney celebrates with members of the Mickey Mouse Club.

1955, *The Mickey Mouse Club* appeared on TV, featuring a cast of young performers called the Mouseketeers. Disney also made TV series of *Zorro* and *Davy Crockett*. These were all huge hits with both kids and adults.

But Disney was not finished with the big screen. He continued to produce all kinds of movies. *Peter Pan*, *Alice in Wonderland*, and *Cinderella* came out in the

Peter Pan tells the story of a boy who never wants to grow up.

early 1950s. They were fully animated. In 1961, a live-action movie called *The Absent-Minded Professor* was released. It is about a professor who invents a kind of rubber that can make things fly.

One of the most famous movies Disney ever made is a combination of live-action and animation called *Mary Poppins*. It was released in 1964. The movie is

Julie Andrews and Dick Van Dyke starred in *Mary Poppins*.

about a London nanny who mysteriously appears to take charge of two young children. Some songs from the movie, such as "Supercalifragilisticexpialidocious" and "A Spoonful of Sugar," are still famous today.

Quick Fact: *Mary Poppins*

Mary Poppins is based on a book by P. L. Travers. The movie was very successful and won awards. But Travers hated the movie's use of live-action and animation. The 2013 movie *Saving Mr. Banks* shows how Disney made the book into a movie.

Disney worked on plans for his theme park, Disneyland, in 1954.

In the early 1950s, Disney wanted to build a huge amusement park near Los Angeles, California. He called it Disneyland, and it opened in 1955. Tourists came from all over the world to visit Disneyland. Disney soon began

Disney's characters have entertained people for more than ninety years.

working on a second park near Orlando, Florida. Walt Disney World opened in 1971.

Walt Disney died on December 15, 1966, in Los Angeles, California. But the Walt Disney Company lives on. Today it is one of the biggest companies in the world. It continues to make cartoons, movies, and TV shows. Mickey Mouse is still one of its most famous and beloved characters. Without Walt Disney, the Walt Disney Company would not exist. He was a pioneer in the field of animation and one of the most successful businessmen of the twentieth century.

TIMELINE

1901 Walt Disney is born on December 5 in Chicago, Illinois.

1906 The Disney family moves to a farm near Marceline, Missouri.

1910 The Disney family moves to Kansas City, Missouri.

1917 The Disney family moves back to Chicago.

1918 Disney drops out of school to drive an ambulance during World War I.

1919 Disney returns from Europe and meets Ub Iwerks.

1922 Disney starts Laugh-O-Gram Films.

1923 Walt and Roy Disney start Disney Brothers Studios.

1925 Disney marries Lillian Bounds.

1927 The first Oswald the Lucky Rabbit cartoon is released.

1928 *Steamboat Willie*, the first cartoon featuring Mickey and Minnie Mouse, is shown in New York City.

1929 Disney Brothers Studios becomes Walt Disney Productions.

1932 *Flowers and Trees*, the first full-color cartoon, is released.

1937 Disney releases *Snow White and the Seven Dwarves*.

1940 Disney releases *Pinocchio*.

1941 Disney animators strike takes place.

1950 *Treasure Island* is released.

1953 *Peter Pan* is released.

1954 *Disneyland* television show airs.

1955 Disneyland opens near Los Angeles, California.

1964 Disney releases *Mary Poppins*.

1966 Walt Disney dies on December 15, in Los Angeles.

1971 Walt Disney World opens near Orlando, Florida.

GLOSSARY

ANIMATION A way of making pictures appear to move. It can be done using drawings, computer graphics, or photographs.

BIG SCREEN Movies and the movie business, especially when they are being compared to television.

BOX OFFICE Term used to describe how many tickets have been sold for a movie.

CHARACTERS People, animals, or other creatures in a story.

FANTASIA A musical composition that does not follow a particular style.

FEATURE-LENGTH FILM A film that is usually between one and three hours long.

ORCHESTRA A group of musicians who play music (usually classical music) together and who are led by a conductor.

PRODUCE To create a movie to present to the public.

STUDIO A major company that produces movies.

THEME PARK Amusement park based on a central theme.

FOR MORE INFORMATION

BOOKS

Green, Sara. *Disney*. Minneapolis, MN: Bellwether Media, Inc., 2015.

Mattern, Joanne. *Walt Disney*. New York, NY: Children's Press, 2013.

Norwich, Grace. *I Am Walt Disney*. New York, NY: Scholastic, 2014.

Orr, Tamra B. *Walt Disney: The Man Behind the Magic*. New York, NY: Scholastic, 2013.

Scollon, Bill. *Walt Disney: Drawn from Imagination*. New York, NY: Disney Press, 2014.

WEBSITES

Because of the changing nature of Internet links, Rosen Publishing has developed an online list of websites related to the subject of this book. This site is updated regularly. Please use this link to access this list:

http://www.rosenlinks.com/BBB/Disney

INDEX